Contents

Acknowledgements

I am grateful to Jean Stogdon, Phillida Sawbridge, David Pitcher, Deborah Cullen, Barbara Hudson, Alexandra Plumtree, Judith Stone and Marion Hundleby for their helpful comments on early drafts. I also want to thank Shaila Shah, BAAF Director of Publications, and her assistant, Jo Francis, for their continuing support and for making their publications look so good. Finally, I am most indebted to all the families who have shared their kinship care experiences with me – without them this handbook could not have been written.

Hedi Argent

BAAF is grateful for the support given by Grandparents plus towards the production of this book.

Supported by **Grandparents plus**

We are delighted to support BAAF on *One of the Family*. Grandparents plus is a young organisation set up in 2002 to improve the recognition and support for grandparents and the extended family in caring for children of the family, thus providing children with continuity of care, culture and heritage, security and self-esteem. Grandparents plus provides training for social workers in kinship care and for grandparents, especially around adoption, and promotes good practice. As a trainer for Grandparents plus, Hedi Argent disseminates the important messages in the book. Further information can be found at www.grandparentsplus.org.uk

One would be in less danger
From the wiles of a stranger
If one's own kin and kith
Were more fun to be with
Ogden Nash

Kin and *kith* and *kinship* are not words we often use, although kinship care has become a familiar term in social work practice. It may therefore be as well to begin this book with definitions from the Oxford English Dictionary.

Kin: A group of persons descended from a common ancestor and so connected by blood relationship; a family, stock, clan.

Kith: The persons who are known; one's friends, fellow countrymen or neighbours.

Kinship: Relationship by descent.

For the purpose of this book, *kinship care* refers to the care given by adult family members or friends to children.

Note about the author

Hedi Argent is an independent adoption consultant, trainer and freelance writer. She is the author of *Find me a Family* (Souvenir Press, 1984), *Whatever Happened to Adam?* (BAAF, 1998), *Related by Adoption* (BAAF, 2004), the co-author of *Taking Extra Care* (BAAF, 1997) and the editor of *Keeping the Doors Open* (BAAF, 1988), *See you Soon* (BAAF, 1995), *Staying Connected* (BAAF, 2002) and *Models of Adoption Support* (BAAF, 2003). She has also written three titles in the children's series published by BAAF: *What Happens in Court?* (2003), *What is Contact?* (2004) and *What is a Disability?* (2004).

Foreword

I have known and sometimes worked with Hedi Argent since we trained as social workers many decades ago; now we are both grandmothers and working together again for Grandparents plus, an organisation set up to promote kinship care, and to offer training and consultation to professionals and extended families.

One of the Family draws on Hedi's knowledge and experience of kinship care, her empathy with families, and her firm belief that children thrive within family networks. Through their own words, children and their grandparents, aunts, uncles and siblings vividly illustrate how children can be sustained by extended family and friends when parental care breaks down – for whatever reason. This handbook for kinship carers also highlights the vital role that social workers, lawyers and voluntary organisations can play in supporting kinship care. Each family is different and needs different solutions. Some will need help in understanding the internet, PlayStation and *Big Brother*; others will need to learn about new teaching methods in schools or new developments in child care. But all kinship networks have much to offer, whether it is pink iced cakes, storytelling or cuddles and reassurance. Without sentimentality, this book celebrates the strength of families and the importance of continuity for the emotional and cultural development of all children.

Whilst *One of the Family* is aimed at kinship carers themselves, providing essential information and practical advice on what is involved and how to get help, it should also be essential reading for all professionals working with families. Kinship care may not always be the cheapest or simplest option for local authorities but, as this book eloquently demonstrates, it can serve the best interests of vulnerable children: we owe it to them to make it work.

Jean Stogdon
Chair, Grandparents plus
April 2005

Introduction

Kinship care has always been with us. There is nothing new about keeping children in the family and in the community. Grannies and grandads, aunties and uncles, adult sisters and brothers and close friends have stepped in at times of family crisis and looked after their nephews and nieces, grandchildren and "godchildren" for a day, a week, a few months or a lifetime. Sometimes relatives give shelter when children are at risk; sometimes they offer stability when the children's home life is chaotic; and sometimes they just enjoy sharing in the care of the family's children.

> **When our Noreen had three little ones all under five, she really needed me. I was like a spare parent for them. I was up there most days or she'd drop them off with me if she had to go anywhere; sometimes she just wanted a rest or I went and did the shopping for her. It made us very close. Even now, when they're all teenagers, they come and see their Nanna; I think it does them good to get away; to have a safe place to go when they're feeling a bit stressed or stroppy. It keeps it in the family.**
> (80-year-old grandmother)

Not all grandparents are as obliging as Nanna above or as readily welcomed by their daughters and sons. Nor can all grandparents spare the time to offer shared care. Very few sit around in rose covered cottages. Most are still working when their grandchildren are born, and they cannot be taken for granted by working mothers as a source of childcare. Grandparents have their own lives, which may not include another dose of childcare. But it can be hard to say "no".

> **I'm afraid if I refuse my daughter would be furious and then she would stop me from seeing my granddaughter.**
> (Grandmother quoted in *The Mail on Sunday*, *You* magazine, July 2000)

Even when relatives have the time to be of help, as extended families have become more dispersed, so kinship childcare arrangements have become more complicated; Mum and Auntie Sis are less likely to be living just around the corner than they once were. Children have increasingly become the sole responsibility of their parents; they are no longer seen as belonging to the wider family, let alone to their community. There is a saying that 'it takes a village to raise a child', but the way most of us live today doesn't promote that kind of mutual support.

After the Second World War, health, education and social services were focused on the nuclear family. Foster care with strangers became the preferred option for children who could not live with their parents. Housing, employment and career opportunities did not encourage the establishment of close extended families. We had to wait for a new Children Act in 1989 (England and Wales) and the Children Acts in Scotland and Northern Ireland in 1995, to reaffirm the importance of keeping children in the family and to encourage the pursuit of kinship care as the placement of first choice. This new legislation was greatly influenced by research evidence about the value of kith and kin (Rowe *et al*, 1984).

The term "kinship care" has come to mean the care given by relatives or friends to children with whom they have an existing relationship. In this sense, "kinship" describes a social network rather than a blood relationship. Neighbours and close friends used to be known to children as "Auntie and Uncle so and so". There was probably no difference in most children's minds between blood and social relations; some were nicer than others but they all belonged in the family circle and were available in time of need. They may not be as available today, they may be spread out over a wider area, and today's children may call everyone by their first names, but the benefits of kinship care are again being acknowledged by government, family rights organisations and child care agencies.

Some minority ethnic groups have a particularly strong tradition of kinship care that has not yet been eroded. "Looking after your own" was often the only way for the tribe, the group, the "race" to survive during periods of oppression, famine or virulent epidemics. When death from disease, persecution and poverty are commonplace, the availability of stand-in parents is essential. Children are all our futures, whatever our background, beliefs or aspirations. Cherishing the children became imperative when the continuation of the nation was at stake, and it remains an integral part of the culture of many minority ethnic groups.

> **I've got five sisters and two brothers all living near. We're a real close family. My two older sisters raised us when Mum died. Our dad was back in Trinidad and he stayed there. It was hard but we managed. We've always managed and we always will. None of us got into trouble or got put into care. Now we've all got our own kids and they're all good kids too. There's not a week goes by without a birthday or family gathering.**
> (Young African Caribbean man)

In the Hawaiian tradition, all the family members of a generation are called sisters or brothers, no matter what the relationship. Some African Caribbean communities do not differentiate between full, half or step-siblings and maintain equally strong family ties with all of them. In traditional Indian culture, the extended family is the important social unit. Two or more related married couples, often of more than one generation, share a home, a common kitchen, and responsibility for all the children.

Today, in many parts of the West, it is expected that young adults will leave home before they find a life partner, that they will create an independent unit and that the State will intervene if they need support. A network of extended family and friends is not necessarily considered essential baggage for successful living. If it were, perhaps kith and kin would also be thought more fun to be with, and Ogden Nash, who wrote the verse quoted at the beginning of this book, would be satisfied.

But kinship placements for children in need of care have become the official preferred option. This has been inspired by practitioners, mainly from the USA, and is supported by new legislation. There is a move to increase the proportion of children placed with families and friends, in order to keep children out of the public care system or, if the law is invoked, to keep them connected to their families and communities. Some social services departments are developing specialist teams and tailoring their services to meet the needs of kinship carers. Many more are planning to do so. In 2003, approximately 78,000 children in the UK were "looked after" by local authorities at any one time. Only about 6,000 of them (England only) were in kinship placements. It is hoped to keep a higher proportion of children with families and friends in the future.

This brief book aims to give families and friends who are kinship carers, or may become kinship carers, information about the choices they can make, the assessment process, the legal framework, the child care system, the support they can expect and the financial help available; it discusses some of the most common problems faced by kinship carers who have to balance the interests of the child, and the child's parents, with their own. Quotes are used throughout the book; unless otherwise stated, they have been taken from personal communications to the author. Names and situations have been changed to preserve anonymity, but the words and the wisdom belong to the kinship carers who are showing the way, and to the children they are looking after.

Why kinship care?

JOHN BIRDSALL PHOTOGRAPHY POSED BY MODELS

Our mum and dad don't know how to cook and that, and they don't ever have any money 'cause they smoke and drink and that, but our gran understands and she can make lovely pink cakes.
(Seven-year-old girl)

Children may be unable to live with their own parents for a variety of reasons. Parents may be too ill to look after their children; they may not be able to keep them safe from physical, emotional or sexual harm; or children may be rejected when parents form new relationships. Some people simply cannot be "good enough" parents, and their children are put at risk through serious neglect or harmed by unsuitable childcare practices. If parents misuse drugs or alcohol, they may not have the necessary reserves of energy or willpower to remain committed to their children. Sometimes a lone parent may be too overwhelmed to manage; sometimes parents who have many children cannot manage to care for all of them; and sometimes parents have to go to prison or become long-stay patients in hospital. More rarely, children lose both their parents in tragic events and become orphans.

A child may need alternative short or long-term care if the parents can't continue to provide it. It's a great help if 'Gran understands', as the little girl says, and if she and her sisters don't have to explain their story to strangers. The 'lovely pink cakes' belonged to this family's tradition and gave the children a sense of continuity and stability when they most yearned for it.

- A kinship carer can be a relative, friend or other person aged 18 or over who is connected to the child.
- The aim of all child care is that children are securely attached to the people who can provide safe and effective care for the duration of their childhood if necessary. The kinship network already has a relationship with the child and has the greatest investment in the child's future.
- Kinship care builds on family strengths even during times of family stress. If some members of the family are in trouble, it doesn't mean that the rest of the family is incapable of taking over; if the extended family is not part of the problem, it may be part of the solution. Sharing responsibility for the family's children can further strengthen the whole family system.

> **We didn't know how close we was
> 'til social services started on about
> putting Kevin in care. We wasn't
> going to let that happen and we
> didn't.**
> (Kinship carer of 15-year-old boy)

- Children who have to suffer the pain of separation and loss will suffer less if they can remain with people they know, people who will keep them feeling connected to their parents and the rest of their family so that they can develop their sense of identity.

> **I just wanted to be with people I
> knew and they knew me. Being
> with my brothers made it better
> and being with my gran made it
> better as well...My mum comes
> round most weekends and my dad,
> he comes at weekends as well.**
> (15-year-old boy quoted in Broad *et al*,
> 2001)

- Kinship care provides an easy route for vital information about the family to reach the child and the carers.
- Children benefit from seeing that their own relatives have made good choices in their lives and are successful partners, parents, workers, providers and carers.

> **When I grow up I'm going out to
> work like my uncle Ned 'cause he
> has enough money and then I can
> give some to my mum.**
> (Eight-year-old boy living with aunt
> and uncle)

- Children feel supported if they share the same religion, culture and ethnicity as their carers – a situation which may be difficult to achieve if they have to live with strangers.

> **You have your own culture and what you believe, so I think it's important to live with someone who knows about it.**
> (Young African Caribbean woman)

- Children will remain the child of one family and not have to adjust to become a child with two families.
- Children find it easier to explain why they live with relatives than why they live with strangers.

> **I just say I live with my nanna and then I don't have to say about being fostered.**
> (From a school project about families by an eight-year-old girl)

- Above all, kinship care may prevent children coming into public care, and shifts the emphasis from family breakdown to family preservation.

The studies of kinship care in the UK are limited, but Bob Broad's work at De Montfort University (2001) comes to clear conclusions: it is better for children to grow up in their own imperfect families than to be placed with more perfect strangers.

2

What's right for you and your family?

JOHN BIRDSALL PHOTOGRAPHY POSED BY MODELS

**When it happened it was so quick
we hardly had time to think, but
we did make the right decision
for them and for us.**
(Woman who fosters her two
nieces aged eight and ten)

Not everyone can bring up children they didn't plan to have. Not everyone has the space in their home or in their life for one unexpected child, let alone several children. Not everyone can commit to child care permanently or – and perhaps this is even more challenging – for an unpredictable length of time. But many people will want to try to respond to a needy child. Sometimes the move to kinship care is gradual: a child or young person may spend increasingly long breaks with a relative before circumstances lead to a permanent arrangement. Unfortunately, if there is an unforeseen crisis in the family, there is hardly ever time to work out what you want to do, what you think you should do and what you really can do.

As I write this, there has been a natural disaster in the Far East. Thousands of people, including tourists, have been killed. Out of all the chaos, one story among many has caught the attention of the media: two brothers of 12 and 15 who were holidaying with their parents have survived, but they have been orphaned, and their distraught aunt is travelling across the world to rescue them. There is no doubt that she is acting as all of us would want to under these conditions, and the public watches and approves.

Rescuing the young from danger of any kind is a very basic response – we share it with all other animals. But unlike other animals, our lives are complicated by the need to make a living, by complex relationships and emotions, by housing conditions and even by transport requirements. How can a family living in the country with two children and a four-seater car afford to exchange it for a bigger one to accommodate two more large boys? Can all the children double up in a three-bedroomed house, or will there have to be a move? Who will support this family arrangement, share the responsibility, and give financial help? What will the rest of the family say and how will existing relationships be affected? If grandparents or other older relatives are taking over, are they really prepared to start parenting all over again? Do they have the health and the stamina?

And we must never forget that when children need kinship care there has usually been a breakdown in the family that affects all its members. Both the children needing care and the potential carers most often share in the same trauma and the carers also have to be looked after.

> Pearl, who was widowed young, was the backbone and the heart and soul of her family. Every Sunday she cooked for her three daughters and their partners and her ten grandchildren. All the family came to Pearl for advice, support and the occasional loan. When her youngest daughter died from an overdose of drugs, the family closed ranks and refused all outside help. They felt shame and guilt because none of them had suspected drug abuse. It was taken for granted that Pearl would take the three children because their father had left the family and remarried abroad. Pearl had a house and had recently retired. The shocked and grieving children moved in with their equally shocked and grieving grandmother. None of them could talk about their loss. The surviving daughters stayed away because Pearl was preoccupied and they were trying to deal with their own pain. Pearl collapsed and was taken to hospital with pneumonia.

The urge to rescue must be followed, or better still preceded, by a plan for management and support. And rescue is not the only motivation for kinship care. Loyalty and love for the child, a sense of family solidarity and the importance of the blood tie are most often foremost when kinship care is offered, but there are also less comfortable driving forces. Stern feelings of obligation and duty may override all practical considerations; grandparents may be driven to compensate for past mistakes with their own children; there may be anger in the family about the way children have been treated by their parents; and an element of "I told you so" can creep in if the children have to be removed from their home. There may also be a temptation to compete in order to be seen as better than the parents. Ideally, family and friends need time to reflect on how and why they are committing to a lifelong role as carers. However, being loved and wanted and welcomed will in the end be more important to children than why or how they came to remain "one of the family".

3

What do the children want and need?

JOHN BIRDSALL PHOTOGRAPHY POSED BY MODELS

I love to know that I belong to somebody, I'm loved by people and it's good to know that I've got somewhere to come after school that I can call home.
(Young person quoted in Broad et al, 2001)

- The most important thing for children is to feel loved, understood, secure, valued and accepted for who they are, rather than how someone would like them to be.
- Children in kinship care want to trust their carers to protect them from whomever has hurt them. If they have had bad experiences, it may take time for them to learn to trust their parents again, or to trust you.
- Most children want to hang on to their parents, even if they can't live with them. Some children fear that they will turn out to be like their parents. If you can show respect and compassion for their parents, it will help the children to feel better about themselves.

> A boy and a girl of 10 and 12 had been sexually exploited by their father in a paedophile ring. They now lived with their paternal grandmother who was bitterly ashamed of her son, but managed to tell the children endearing stories about his childhood. 'I had five boys', she said, 'and your dad was the best of the bunch.'

- If children have been separated from siblings, they will need reassurance that they are not inferior to children still living with their parents or placed in other families, and that none of what has happened is their fault.
- Continuity is vital to all of us. It is particularly easy for children to lose the thread of their story. Keeping in touch with parents, sisters, brothers, the wider family and friends, and holding absent people in mind, will enable children to remain connected to their past, to live in the present and to look forward to the future.

> **I sleep in my mum's old room now. She likes that. So do I.**
> (Five-year-old boy living with grandparents)

- Belonging is an idea, a concept that has nothing to do with possession. Neither the parents nor the carers own a child. Children will feel that they belong if they are growing up with a secure place in the family circle, and are included in the family traditions and stories. Grandparents hold the longest memory and are often great storytellers.

> **My "gramp" remembers things he tells me about when I was a baby, so I won't forget and he knows stories about my mum when she was little...**
> (Five-year-old boy living with grandparents)

- It is essential for children to know who is in charge and who is making decisions about them. They need to understand the roles, responsibilities and authority the adults have in relation to them and to each other. It can be scary for a child to feel that their life is spinning out of control or that the adults around them can't co-operate. Children may play parents and carers off against each other if they find themselves at the centre of hostility, or they might try and "take over" and be labelled as "controlling".
- Children want to be clear about why they cannot live with their parents and whether they may, at some time in the future, return to them. If they are not allowed to see their parents, they will require an honest explanation or they may, in rare cases, be reassured.

> **I was scared that my mum would get me any time she wanted before the court. After the court we had a party.**
> (Child in kinship care, quoted in Pitcher, 1999)

- It will make the child more confident if everyone in the family tells the truth and the same story in a sympathetic way – even if it's a painful story. But children also have a right to privacy and probably need help with describing their situation to others.

> **My auntie says to tell people I live with her because my mum is sick, and then I don't have to explain anything else. But me and her know all about it.**
> (Seven-year-old girl)

- When family boundaries are blurred, it can be confusing for children to know what they should call their kinship carers. It is not helpful if aunties, uncles and grandparents, or other relatives or friends of the family, become "Mum" and "Dad". It is better for everyone if children can remain rooted in the reality of their situation. It also paves the way for eventual reunification with parents if that is at all possible.

> **This child is my grandchild now and forever. He calls me "grandma"... I'm his grandparent, not his parent. It would just confuse everything to pretend I'm his parent...Besides, I don't want to take away my son's parental rights. I live in the hope that one of these days he'll get over those drug problems.**
> (Kinship carer, quoted in McFadden, 1995)

- Children want to know the rules – what is and what is not allowed and what happens if the rules are broken? In Bob Broad *et al*'s (2001) study, *Kith and Kin*, teenagers in kinship care related that they were given less freedom and less pocket money than their friends, but staying in the family was more important. Each family has different rules and routines and most of them work if they are benign and consistent.

> **We always ate on our lap watching
> the TV at home. I wasn't used to
> eating at the table, but I'm used to
> it now.**
> (10-year-old girl living with her aunt)

- Children would prefer to grow up healthy and well educated –
  they may not want to do their homework or they may not like
  vegetables, but they wouldn't thank us if we ignored their
  education and well-being. A child may measure your
  commitment by your interest in school and health matters.
  Attending school open days, concerts, teachers' forums, prize
  and sports days, and balancing the fruit/sweets intake is
  evidence of caring.
- Children want to be heard; they want their feelings to be
  accepted; they want to have their non-verbal messages
  understood. We are learning more about children's emotional
  needs and about childhood disabilities like ADHD (Attention
  Deficit Hyperactivity Disorder). We no longer say 'what's a
  child got to be depressed about?' or 'he'd better learn to sit
  still!' Check out how you're doing: can you put yourself in a
  child's shoes? Can you think with a child's mind? Can you
  feel a child's joy and pain?
- Even if, for whatever reason, it is not possible to keep children
  in the family, it will be important for them to know that you
  tried and that they were wanted.

Parenting again?

JOHN BIRDSALL PHOTOGRAPHY POSED BY MODELS

**My nan isn't really old – she looks
a bit old but she isn't.**
(Child in nursery class)

Even if you have brought up a family already, parenting for the second time around entails a change of gear. All people have to adjust when children are born to them but most parents, however vaguely, have included children in their life expectations. Grandparents and older relatives have usually put their childcaring days behind them.

It is emotionally and physically demanding to look after infants, school-aged children or adolescents full time. Even young parents complain about lack of sleep, are preoccupied about behaviour and education, and worry about sex and drugs. Grandparents are famous for enjoying their grandchildren because they can hand them back to the parents when they have had enough. Looking after a toddler – and probably "spoiling" him – one day a week or every day for a couple of hours after school, is very different from having the main responsibility for day-to-day care. Dreams of taking it easy and gentle holidays in the sun during school terms when holidays are cheaper and destinations less crowded will have to give way to routines of getting up early, three wholesome meals a day, packed lunches, taking and collecting, homework, playing snakes and ladders over and over again, rough and tumbles with aching joints, answering endless questions, telling endless stories, watching endless cartoons, tripping over toys, making sandcastles, getting cold in the playground, getting children to bed and, later, having the phone and the bathroom permanently engaged, having arguments over just about everything and waiting up anxiously until they get home. Or, if grandparents are still working, childminders can be expensive and may be hard to find.

> **What social life? Your friends don't want to know about toilet training and that kind of thing. They've been there and done that! They can't believe I'm back to babysitters and baby food. I never thought I'd get so involved again. But to tell you the truth, I wouldn't change**

> **one day of my life now for all that
> leisure I was so looking forward to.**
> (Lone grandmother caring for a two-
> year-old child)

Parenting again does not mean doing the same all over again. Times
change and childcare practices have changed even more quickly. My
grandmother taught my mother to knit, crochet, embroider and to
make her own clothes. I barely managed to take hems up and down
and knit baby clothes and I didn't manage to teach my own children
much more than how to sew on a button. I don't believe that my
grandchildren can thread a needle. It isn't simply a question of
losing skills but a matter of changing needs.

Television, computer games, "takeaways", mobile phones,
PlayStations, supermarkets, cheap air travel and designer labels are
transforming our children's lives.

> **He doesn't like what I have bought.
> He only wants things with labels. I
> want him to buy a suit, but he's not
> interested. I told him to buy proper
> shoes. He will only wear trainers...**
> (Grandparent carer of teenager quoted
> in Broad et al, 2001)

When my children were 15 it was not unreasonable to tell them
when to be home. My granddaughter, aged 15, rings on the mobile
to tell *us* when she will be home. It is not possible to monitor what
children see on television today because, even if they don't have a
TV in their room, one of their friends will. It is possible to block
some unsuitable sites on the internet, but the friend's parents might
not bother. Children have become more knowing and more
streetwise. They reach adolescence sooner and remain adolescents
for longer.

It can be hard for grandparents and older relatives to adjust to a new
way of bringing up children. And should they really try to, or was

the old way good enough? On the one hand, children like to conform; they do not like to be different from their peers. If their friends are allowed to stay out late, to play on the street, to watch *Eastenders*, to have their ears treble-pierced, to wear the latest gear – this list has no end – then they will feel hard done by if they can't. But, on the other hand, if children feel "one of the family", they may adjust to old ways more readily than their grandparents will accept the new.

> **My Nanna and Pop are old-fashioned. They are very strict. They treat me like when my mum was little. But they are very kind and I really love them, and my friends like coming because Nanna gives them nice teas and Pop is a joker. I've nearly always lived with them and I don't ever want them to die.**
> (Nine-year-old girl living with grandparents)

This little girl may not feel quite as happy about her 'old-fashioned' grandparents if her social life becomes restricted when she is a teenager.

> **Nan is an older class person so she says it's not right for boys to go round touching girls and that. So if I have a girlfriend, then I have to go out.**
> (16-year-old quoted in Broad *et al*, 2001)

And it can be rewarding for "oldies" to keep up with the youngsters.

> **We realise how fortunate we are not to have lost our grandchildren to strangers as so many have. We have become highly qualified in *Bob the Builder*, PlayStation,**

> **Beyblades, Motown, Xbox, *Pop Idol*
> and *Big Brother*. And we're the ones
> who get all the cuddles, dry the
> tears, and steer them into
> adulthood.**
> (Grandparent caring for two
> granddaughters)

However, there are some changes in raising children that are more important than rules and knowing about the latest craze. "Not in front of the children" used to be said, and thought, in order to protect them from painful truths and unsuitable information. It was presumed that children should not be burdened with adult concerns. Sex was almost a taboo subject. Drugs, alcohol, domestic violence and mental health were better not spoken about. Family secrets were kept from the children. Consequently, many young people grew up in ignorance of true family relationships: some believed that kinship carers were their parents, and that their mother was their sister or their aunt.

Today there is a greater spirit of openness. Children have a right to know who they are, and why they are where they are. They deserve truthful answers to their questions and the encouragement to ask those questions. It is difficult to talk openly to a maturing girl about a mother who sleeps with men to fund her drug habit, or to talk to a boy about his abusive father, but it is easier for children to grow up knowing the truth, than it is for them to fantasise and be confused or scared by what cannot be spoken about. And family secrets have a habit of hovering in the air and bursting out at the most inconvenient moment.

> **First of all I thought the people I
> lived with were my mum and dad.
> Then, when I was nine, I found out
> they were my aunt and uncle and
> that they wanted to adopt me. But
> my real mother, my aunt's sister,
> who I'd always thought till then**

> **was another auntie, wouldn't agree
> to it so I never got adopted. Then,
> when I was 14, it all came out that
> my uncle was also my dad and
> there was this great row and I was
> turned out and put into care. I
> never saw any of them again.**
> (Man born between the two world
> wars)

Contrast that sad story with Angela's account of kinship care.

> **I always knew why I couldn't live
> with my mother and that no one
> really knew who my dad was. I
> could always talk to my grandma
> and sometimes we'd cry together
> over my mum. I never felt she kept
> anything from me. I was never
> worried about finding a skeleton in
> the cupboard.**
> (Angela, aged 20)

Another important change in social attitudes, backed by legislation, has affected every aspect of child care, including kinship care. It is no longer permissible to smack a child that is not your own, and even if it is your own, you must not smack hard enough to leave a mark. There has been, and still is, a great deal of controversy about whether or not a smack does any harm. Most adults today can remember being smacked for good reasons – perhaps a smack on the hand was used to emphasise a firm "no"; unfortunately, many can also remember feeling assaulted and being physically abused. Unless we are seriously disturbed, we do not go around hitting out at other adults if they happen to behave in a way that displeases us. It does seem unfair to use force on children who are less able to defend themselves – and what does it teach them?

Current trends may feel like a criticism of the way older people have brought up their own families. It may be hard to let go of convictions about discipline and good behaviour, especially if the child's parents have been unable to do well and the grandparents think they know better. Each generation has its own set of values; some are carried forward and some are rejected by the next. How often do we hear people say, 'I do it just like my mum did,' or, 'I do everything in the opposite way to my mum'? In kinship care the generations can become indistinct and the "generation gap" can widen. We have to mind that we help children to bridge that gap by meeting them at least halfway.

> **To begin with we did everything the same as we'd done with our own. I suppose we were more confident that way. And she was good; she did as she was asked but she sort of went inside herself. When we loosened up a bit, she did too. It's more of a give-and-take now: she listens to us and we try to be more modern.**
> (Older kinship carers)

> **I help them to understand what game I'm playing and they help me to read.**
> (Eight-year-old boy living with grandparents)

5

Starting from scratch or adding on?

JOHN BIRDSALL PHOTOGRAPHY POSED BY MODELS

> I never thought I'd have any children and I didn't miss them, but when it came to it, there was no question in my mind. I went in at the deep end and had to do my learning as I went along.
> (Single kinship carer)

Childless relatives and friends may have either chosen to remain that way, may be unable to have children, or may have their own personal plan for parenthood. They may regard a kinship placement as a blessing. Or they may not.

> Sophie had recently married and was planning to get pregnant as quickly as possible. Her twin sister, who had always been unstable and made unreasonable demands on her, became pregnant first and gave birth to a healthy child. She was uncertain who the father was. She abandoned the child with Sophie and went abroad without leaving an address. The twin's parents were dead and there were no other close relatives. Sophie's husband didn't want his sister-in-law's child because he feared hereditary mental illness, and Sophie felt that if they kept the baby, her marriage and the child's security would be threatened by her sister's erratic interference. They decided to let their local authority take responsibility for placing the baby with strangers.

Kinship care will not fit into every family's life story and it is sometimes harder to say "no" than it is to say "yes". But it is possible to say "no", and it may be necessary to say "no" for the sake of the child as well as for the sake of the family.

Whether you have experience of bringing up children or not, becoming a kinship carer will change your life. Most people have at least a few months to prepare for parenthood, and they usually start with a baby. But kinship care is nearly always unexpected; it may involve several children of different ages; and often begins in dramatic circumstances, which affect the carers as well as the children.

Adding a child or children to an existing family group can strain emotional and physical resources. Fitting children together can be upsetting for all of them. New children may feel second-best and "homegrown" children may feel ousted. It is essential to include all of them, depending on age and level of understanding, in family discussions and plans about the changed situation.

If childless people take an infant, it may upset their work/leisure balance. If they take an older child, or more than one, they will have to catch up on a lot of experience very quickly. And how do you learn to be a consistent, stand-in parent to a 12-year-old when you have previously been an occasional, fond, indulgent auntie?

> **I used to tell my sister not to bother about Jade's room being so untidy. They had a constant battle about it and it affected their relationship. But now she's with me, and it's my house, I've taken on the battle because I can't stand the mess.**
> (Single kinship carer of 12-year-old girl)

Few kinship carers are left entirely on their own. Statutory agencies are likely to be involved; financial help could be available; there may be court proceedings; there will nearly always be meetings, reports and visits from social workers. It can feel overwhelming to have to deal with officialdom while trying to get on with your life and settling distressed children who will need more than the normal amount of attention. But agencies are beginning to train specialists in kinship care and their support could well be worth having.

6

Staying together or living apart?

JOHN BIRDSALL PHOTOGRAPHY POSED BY MODELS

Siblings should not be separated when in care or when looked after under voluntary arrangements, unless this is part of a well thought out plan based on each child's needs.
(Department of Health guidance to the 1989 Children Act (England and Wales))

Sibling relationships can be complicated – half-brothers and sisters and step-brothers and sisters can be as important to a child as full siblings. Children who share a childhood and grow up together could have the longest and closest relationship of their lives with each other. Even some children separated in infancy say that they have never let go of their sibling in their mind.

Kinship carers, who are motivated to keep the family together, may face a dilemma about separating one or two or more children from their sisters and brothers. If the oldest child of a young mother lives with her grandparents, while subsequent children stay with the mother and her new partner, how will these children relate to each other? What will it mean to the child in kinship care if a brother or a sister is being fostered by strangers or has been adopted? Is it better to keep one child in the family if you can't keep them all? Should a large group of children be split between various members of a family? Or if grandparents look after the first child of a daughter with learning disabilities, do they have to commit themselves to take any other children she might have?

> Kate adopted Margaret, a girl of five, with a severe learning disability. When Margaret was 16, she had a relationship with an older man and became pregnant. Kate had no hesitation in taking on the permanent care of the baby while helping Margaret to be as involved as possible. Two years later Margaret moved out of the family home and immediately became pregnant again. Social services approached Kate about taking the second child. Kate now has both children but she is adamant that she cannot take any more.

Clearly, each case has to be judged according to the circumstances, the children's attachment to each other, their wishes and feelings, and the capacity of the carers. It has to be possible to say "enough", but it is vital to be aware of the significance of staying together or living apart.

Whether you and your family have time to come to an informed decision, or whether you have to make up your mind in a crisis, there are several routes to take along the kinship care way.

7

What are the choices?

JOHN BIRDSALL PHOTOGRAPHY POSED BY MODELS

> We wanted to look after the twins
> permanently – just, you know,
> look after them like we had
> before whenever they needed us.
> But we had to go to court and in
> the end we didn't know where we
> were or what was expected.
> We've got them now but it took a
> long time to sort it out.
> (Aunt and uncle of twins)

There are many different ways of keeping children in the family when they can't live with their parents. Relatives and friends often care for children, if the need arises, without any support or intervention from education, health or social services. We can't even know how many children are looked after informally because there are no records of private arrangements. Even if outside agencies are involved in making the initial kinship placements, the family may choose not to use any services that are offered. But if children are deemed to be at risk of harm, or if there is conflict and litigation, more formal and secure arrangements may have to be made in order to protect both children and carers. The details of these arrangements will vary according to the laws of Scotland, Northern Ireland, England and Wales, but the principles of kinship care are essentially the same throughout the UK. All kinship carers and potential kinship carers should be clear about the options that could be available to them and the regulations that apply to them.

- **Informal family arrangements**, in keeping with the parents' wishes, are a private affair, and can remain so as long as children are not put at risk. The parents retain full parental responsibility (responsibilities in Scotland). The children and their kinship carers have the same rights to services as all children and carers in the community have.

> Jamie and Josh were full brothers. Their father left the family before Josh was born and did not stay in touch. Their mother suffered from seriously disabling, recurring bouts of depression. The boys' maternal aunt, who lived in the same street with her husband and three children, regularly took Jamie and Josh into her own home whenever her sister was ill. By the time both boys were in secondary school, their mother was permanently hospitalised and they became wholly dependent on their aunt. Josh had special educational needs and was given extra help at school. The aunt successfully applied to social services for financial help with holidays and school uniforms.

- **Private foster care** with friends has to be notified to the local authority within specified time limits. Social services have a duty to assess, to carry out certain checks, and to visit in line with regulations. They also have the power to remove a child from unsuitable situations. The parents retain full parental responsibility (responsibilities in Scotland).

> Jasmine, aged 14, refused to live at home when her mother's new boyfriend moved in, so she went to stay at a friend's house. After a week the friend's parents told Jasmine that she could stay for as long as she wanted, if her mum agreed and helped out financially. Private arrangements were made. The school advised the friend's parents to inform the local authority. A social worker visited regularly and was available if Jasmine or either family needed her. Jasmine stayed with her private foster carers for nearly a year.

- The local authority may have been asked to **accommodate** children because they cannot stay at home. If there is no identified risk to the children, the local authority will not need to take any formal proceedings. Kinship care, with the parents' consent, should be explored as the first placement choice. There may be no further social services involvement unless the carers ask to be assessed as kinship foster carers. The parents retain full parental responsibility (responsibilities in Scotland).

> A hospital sister called social services to say that a young mother had given birth to a boy with Down's Syndrome and had abandoned the child in hospital. The social worker traced the mother who asked for the child to be accommodated by the local authority while she sorted herself out. With the mother's permission, the social worker contacted the maternal grandmother, who agreed to look after the baby. An assessment was completed and the baby stayed with the grandmother. The family wanted to manage on their own and the local authority withdrew.

• The possibility of **kinship foster care** must be considered first by the local authority, if the court (in England and Wales) or the Children's Hearing System (in Scotland) has made an Order requiring the child to reside away from home. Social services have a duty to assess, maintain, support and supervise all foster carers. In an emergency, and if the local authority believes that a placement with kinship carers is in the child's best interests, the placement can go ahead immediately but the carer must agree, in writing, to abide by conditions to protect the child. A local authority assessment, to include the child's wishes and feelings, must be completed within a specified period. A **permanency** or **fostering panel** has to be involved in the approval of all foster carers. The local authority and the parents share parental responsibility in England and Wales; in Scotland, the parents retain full parental responsibilities.

Five-year-old Kalil was removed from home following a non-accidental injury. He was placed with emergency foster carers while the local authority applied to the court for a Care Order. An Interim Care Order was granted and a social worker was appointed. It was unlikely that Kalil would be able to return to his parents and the local authority was directed to find a permanent placement for him and to present a Care Plan to the court. The social worker organised a Family Group Conference. Kalil's extended family decided that Kalil should live with his paternal grandparents and two adult uncles. The grandparents wanted to have the continued backing and support of the local authority in order to manage contact with Kalil's parents and to protect him from further harm. They also needed a regular fostering allowance. Kalil was placed with his grandparents while the social worker made an assessment with the help of an interpreter. The grandparents were approved by the fostering panel and Kalil grew up in their care. He remained a looked after child on a full Care Order until he was 18.

- It may be that the local authority considers that kinship carers require formal support or **supervision** for a limited or trial period.

> Two teenage sisters and their younger brother were left on their own in the north Midlands when their mother died of a drugs overdose. They were accommodated by the local authority and placed together in a children's home while their father and other relatives in London were contacted. The father was physically disabled and could not look after his children on his own but there were many aunts, uncles and adult cousins on both sides of the family who lived nearby and were eager to help. There was a strong belief that "families should look after their own". It was agreed that the children would live with their father and an older aunt if they could transfer together to a larger flat. The family situation was assessed and references had to be checked for all the people who would be involved with the children's care. The father was given a four-bedroomed flat. The local authority applied to the court for a one year Supervision Order with the agreement of the family. The father now had sole parental responsibility.

- Kinship carers can apply to the court for a **Residence Order**, which gives them shared parental responsibility with the parents until the child is 16. (In England and Wales, in special circumstances, this can last until the child is 18.) It also means that the child will not be "in care". Although the local authority has no statutory duty under a Residence Order, agreements for support, including financial support, can be negotiated.

> Donna was brought up by her grandmother from birth because her teenage mother, Margaret, had severe learning disabilities. When Margaret was 18, she left home and took no further interest in Donna. The grandmother wanted to secure Donna's position and to have some official parental responsibility. She applied to the court and was granted a Residence Order.

- **Special Guardianship Orders** are to be introduced in England and Wales at the end of 2005 (legislation will follow in Northern Ireland). They are similar to Residence Orders but give the carers primary parental responsibility, and do not expire until the child is 18. In addition, the local authority has the power to provide special guardianship support services, including financial support. Before making a Special Guardianship Order, the court must have a report from the local authority.

> If Special Guardianship Orders had been in force when Margaret (above) left home, Donna's grandmother might have chosen to apply for one. It would have secured Donna's placement until she was 18, and have allowed her grandmother to make decisions in Margaret's absence.

- It is possible for family members to adopt related children. This is not a step to be taken lightly as it can distort relationships and confuse the generations. However, there are situations when an **Adoption Order** offers a child the greatest stability. The court and local authority are involved in all adoptions. The new adoptive parents hold full parental responsibility and the birth parents lose theirs.

> The parents of 10-year-old Michael were killed in a road accident. He was immediately included in his uncle's family. When he was 12, his uncle and aunt said that they would like to adopt him so that he would have the same rights as their other children and they would have official parental responsibility. Michael agreed and was pleased that his name would remain the same. The whole family supported the adoption plan. A social worker wrote a report for the court and Michael was adopted.

- Parents (and Special Guardians) can name a **legal guardian** to take their place if they die. The appointment can be, but does not have to be, included in a will. It must be in writing and signed and dated. If the child's parents are dead and there is no one else with parental responsibility for the child, it is possible for relatives or friends to apply to the court to become a child's guardian (this is not to be confused with applying for a Special Guardianship Order).

> Maria, a widow with five children, dropped dead suddenly while working as a home help. The oldest daughter, Sonya, was 18. The other children were aged eight to 14. With the help of her social worker, Sonya became the younger children's legal guardian. Although social services were heavily involved in supporting Sonya, the family stayed intact.

What does it all mean?

JOHN BIRDSALL PHOTOGRAPHY POSED BY MODELS

**We didn't know what had hit us!
One moment we were looking
after our grandchildren, and the
next we were surrounded by
social workers, forms and jargon
we didn't understand.**
(Grandparents of two young children)

As soon as official agencies become involved in family life, official people, terms, forms and documents creep into the process. It's as well to know what is what and who is who, so that there is no confusion or mystery.

- **Parental responsibility (parental reponsibilities** in Scotland) gives the holder the authority and the duty to act on the child's behalf, which includes making day-to-day decisions, giving consent to medical treatment (unless the child is old enough to do so), and deciding on schools. If parental responsibility is shared, the other parties have to be consulted.
- **Looked after children** are all children who are looked after by the local authority, either with the agreement of their parents or under an Order.
- **Accommodated children** are looked after by the local authority at the request of, or agreement with, the child's parents.
- **A child in need** is any child in the community who has an identified need for special services. The local authority has a duty to assess if a referral is made.
- **Care and Supervision Orders or Requirements** are made in favour of a local authority when it can be shown that a child has suffered, or is at risk of suffering, significant harm if the Order is not made. In Scotland a Supervision Requirement is made by the Children's Hearing and reviewed annually or more frequently.
- **Residence Orders and Special Guardianship Orders** give legal status and authority to an arrangement that is in the child's best interests. In general, they are used to confirm and safeguard existing arrangements. They entitle the carer to participate in all major decisions about residence, education and medical treatment (unless the child is old enough to sign consent) but do not entitle them to change the child's surname without agreement or a court order.
- **Adoption Orders** are made by the court when it is evident that a child needs permanent new parents. The adopted child

has the same status as children born to the adoptive parents.
- **Prohibited Steps and Specific Issues Orders** can be made to meet a child's identified needs. For instance, it may be necessary to prevent a person from visiting the child or it may be necessary for the child to have a particular medical treatment. In Scotland, there are no Prohibited Steps or Specific Issues Orders.
- **Contact Orders** can be made in England and Wales in conjunction with an Order for care if a local authority requests that contact should either be prescribed or terminated. In England and Wales, relatives may apply for a Contact Order, with the leave of the court, to gain contact with a child; if they hold a Residence Order, they can apply to regulate or limit contact. In Scotland, anyone claiming an interest, including relatives, can apply for Contact Orders.
- **Family Group Conferences** should be held to enable the wider family to participate in decisions about a child's future. They are a very important development in childcare practice and will be discussed further in the next chapter of this book.
- **Permanency, fostering or adoption panels** are made up of medical advisors, councillors, social workers and independent members, including service users. They have to make recommendations to the agency about the suitability of every proposed placement of a looked after child.
- A **legal guardian** has full powers to act on behalf of a child in place of the parents.
- The **child's social worker** is appointed by the local authority whenever a child becomes looked after.
- The **supervising social worker** or **link worker** is appointed by the local authority to support the carers if a child is fostered.
- A **Children's Guardian** (in England and Wales) or **Curator *ad litem*** (in Scotland) is an independent social worker appointed to protect the interests of the child in some proceedings. She or he must interview all parties, write a

report and appoint a solicitor to act on behalf of the child.
• A **party to the proceedings** is anyone who is directly involved
  in a legal case. Relatives or friends of a child can be given
  permission to become "parties".

This sounds a lot to take in, but not all of it will concern you and
help is at hand. Social workers don't want to make it hard for
kinship carers although they may be under pressure to find the best
solution for a child. Local authority legal departments are there to
enable, not to obstruct. On the whole, kinship care placements can
be arranged without resorting to the law. However, sometimes it is
necessary to disagree and to seek outside advice. Financial aid may
be available (depending on income) through Community Legal
Services (formerly Legal Aid in England and Wales) or through
Legal Aid (in Scotland); solicitors on the Children Panel have the
expertise to steer carers or potential carers safely through the
system. The local Citizens Advice Bureau will have a list of
solicitors on the panel. You can represent yourself in court if you
wish – it can seem daunting, but court officials are usually very
helpful.

A local authority applied for an Order to allow a newborn
infant, named Cheryl, to be placed for adoption. The baby's
mother, Janice, was a heroin addict and the child was born
with drug withdrawal syndrome. The maternal grandmother
opposed the adoption plan and applied to the local authority
to become a kinship carer. Cheryl was placed with "stranger"
foster carers while the grandmother's situation was assessed.
The assessment concluded that the grandmother would be
unable to keep Cheryl safe from Janice and confirmed the
adoption plan. The Curator *ad litem*, appointed by the court,
supported the view of the local authority.

The grandmother took legal advice, opposed the local
authority, and applied for a Residence Order with a Contact
Order to regulate the contact between her daughter and
granddaughter. She was made a party to the proceedings. The
court directed the local authority to conduct an independent

assessment of the grandparent and the risks involved if Cheryl were placed with her. This second assessment recommended that the baby should be placed with the grandmother, that the local authority should give intensive support to Janice and that the grandmother was capable of supervising prescribed contact between Cheryl and her mother. The local authority, with the encouragement of the Curator *ad litem*, also reassessed the situation and made a provisional plan for kinship care with the grandmother.

The court granted a Residence Order and made a Contact Order for one afternoon a week. Cheryl remained a child of the family and grew up knowing her mother, although Janice was never able to look after her.

What exactly is a Family Group Conference?

JOHN BIRDSALL PHOTOGRAPHY POSED BY MODELS

> When we all got together we realised what a lot we had to offer David and how important we were for him. He could have gone into care, but we kept him in the family.
> (Member of Family Group Conference)

Family Group Conferences (FGCs) originated in New Zealand as a method of involving the kinship network when plans have to be made for a child's care and safety. They are based on the belief that the network has the greatest understanding about its own strengths, resources and weaknesses, and knows best what goes on in the family. The role of the professional in FGCs is to facilitate the family decision-making process.

Agencies in the UK have become increasingly interested in developing this model when there is a decision that a looked after child needs to be placed in a permanent substitute family. The use of FGCs meets the legal requirement to consult the family and to explore the resources a family can offer. Families can easily feel excluded when long-term childcare decisions are made; it can be frustrating for the family and devastating for the child if possibilities unknown to professionals are never recognised.

FGCs are not a way to cut costs by using family resources. Families may negotiate plans that professionals had not considered, but these plans will need both practical assistance and funding. The plans produced will vary in style, scope and costs according to the particular needs of the child. Good plans will reflect issues of ethnicity, religion and culture, and move away from court-dominated procedures.

There are different ways of including families in decision-making, but the aims should always be the same.

- To enable parents, carers, relatives and other significant adults to come together and feel entitled to make decisions which will be in the best interests of children when there are child protection concerns or when a child is, or might otherwise be, accommodated.
- To build a greater level of support for young people aged 16–18 who are leaving home and may be at risk.
- To reduce the need for accommodation with strangers and for Court Orders.

- To enhance the likelihood of rehabilitation with parents or placement within the kinship network.
- To promote positive partnerships between families and social services departments.
- To empower people from minority ethnic groups who may experience difficulties in dealing with a predominantly "other" organisation. (Translation/interpretation services should be made available.)

The Family Rights Group (see Useful organisations) has developed a style of FGC, which consists of four stages.

1. Following a referral about a child that cannot be easily resolved, the FGC co-ordinator is notified and, after consultation and negotiation with parents, carers and social workers, invites the kinship network to attend an FGC. The child or children can also attend if they wish, and can bring an advocate of their choice.
2. At the beginning of the meeting, the relevant professionals share their knowledge of the case, their views and concerns, and answer any questions put to them.
3. The professionals, including the co-ordinator, withdraw, leaving the kinship group to make a plan for the child or children.
4. When the family has formulated a plan, the social workers rejoin the meeting and agree any necessary professional involvement. The kinship plan should be acted upon unless it is the professional view that it places a child at risk of significant harm.

> **The organiser visited us and explained it all to us so that we knew what to expect. The first part was quite formal. They told us what they knew and what they thought and what they wanted us to do. When they left us to ourselves no one wanted to take the lead and it**

was a bit stressful. Then Grandpa said how they wanted to have Anna and Maggie, but how they were looking to the rest of us to help out. My sister was worried about them taking on too much at their age but then everyone suggested ways of giving them a hand. In the end we'd planned it all out and it was a really enjoyable family gathering like we normally only have at Christmas. The social workers just accepted everything we said – they've put in extras here and there, and it's worked out fine.
(Anna's and Maggie's uncle)

The role of the co-ordinator is crucial in this model. She or he must not be involved in the case, and should preferably be independent, or at least be specially trained to handle all FGCs for the agency. Decisions have to be made about who is included in the kinship network; it is clear that there may be people who cannot contribute to planning for a child because of the risks they pose. Whether and how best to include children in the meeting has to be sensitively negotiated. There are practical issues like transport, and providing a comfortable room and refreshments to sustain a large group through a lengthy process. It is quite usual for FGCs to take a whole day or even longer. The co-ordinator must prepare all the people attending, to ensure that the conference is able to produce effective and realistic plans. If the family is dissatisfied with the process or the outcome, complaints should, in the first place, be addressed to the co-ordinator.

There is no hard and fast rule about how kinship networks should be involved in making decisions. Any method that allows extended families to be heard is good for children. Sometimes conferences can be on a smaller scale or be held at different stages.

If you are thinking about becoming a kinship carer, and if you have not already been invited to an FGC, you can ask your social services department to organise one if you think it would be helpful. If there was an FGC before you became a kinship carer, you may think it time to have another one to sort out any problems that have arisen in the meantime. Not every local authority has taken up the practice of involving the wider family in a decision-making conference, but families, as well as social workers, can lead the way.

Daniel, aged seven, had to be removed from his parents after he was admitted to hospital in London with serious non-accidental injuries. There was a large extended family on both sides, living in the Midlands; two of the mother's brothers and one of the father's sisters contacted the London borough with offers to look after Daniel. Social services appointed an independent social worker in the Midlands to decide which of the applications to pursue. The social worker invited the uncles, their wives and older children, and the single aunt to come and discuss Daniel's future together. There was a unanimous decision to proceed with one of the uncles. The assessment was very positive. The social worker then set up a conference with all members of both families to make decisions about contact, short breaks, holidays and support needs.

What are assessments for?

I said I wanted to keep Ayesha in the family and they went and did an assessment of me. It was a young lady social worker and she treated me like I was asking to "ordinary" foster for them. She knew Ayesha was my granddaughter but it made no difference.

(Prospective kinship carer)

Relatives and friends, who may already be looking after the children needing care, could think it odd that they have to be assessed to become formal kinship carers, especially as so many informal arrangements never come to the attention of official agencies. It can be hard for family members to find the right balance between protecting the family's privacy and giving all the information necessary. However, a good assessment should not only fulfil legal requirements but also help kinship carers to take stock of their capacities, to be open and honest about any uncertainties and to focus on the child's needs. Working together on an assessment with social services may be seen as a measure of taking the child's welfare seriously.

An assessment of kinship carers should be no less thorough than an assessment of strangers, but it is important to establish the differences at the very beginning. Apart from making sure that the child will be wanted, respected, educated, nurtured and secure, there are some issues specific to kinship care. Your existing relationships with the child and the child's parents are central.

- How comfortable does the child feel with you? Do you agree that the child should be separated from the parents? How will your relationship with the child's parents be affected? How will the rest of the family react if the child lives with you?
- There is a danger in kinship placements that children can get cut off from one side of their family – most often the father's side. How will you make sure that the child stays connected to both sides of their family if at all possible?
- How will you handle conflicts, loyalties, rivalries and alliances that may divide the family as relationships change?
- If the parents are said to have abused the child, do you believe it and can you keep the child safe? If you are angry with the parents, can you avoid displacing your feelings onto the child?
- If your partner is not related to the child, how does she or he view the kinship care plan?
- How will you handle contact between the child and the child's

parents? Will you want the child to return to the parents if circumstances change?

- Is there anything regarding ethnicity or religion or sexual orientation that would get in the way of the placement? Relatives may need to discuss their views if the children are of a different ethnicity or religion, or if one of the parents is lesbian or gay.
- If your own children got into trouble, how will kinship care be different?

Ruby was brought up by her grandmother in the Caribbean. She came to England to join her parents when she was a teenager. She couldn't settle, left home, had a child, Jody, and suffered a series of mental breakdowns. Jody had many moves in and out of foster care whenever her mother was hospitalised. She was described as an aggressive, wilful child.

When Jody was 12, Ruby married, had two more children, took a college course, held down a responsible job, and became deeply religious. She had no further episodes of mental illness and the two younger children were healthy and made good progress.

But Jody, in the meantime, was getting increasingly out of control. She truanted from school and alternated between making unrealistic demands on her mother and rejecting her completely. When she was 15, she refused to live at home and was accommodated by the local authority. She became pregnant but would not name the father, or agree to being placed with the baby in a residential assessment centre. After the baby was born, Jody disappeared from the hospital. She contacted Ruby and asked her to take the baby. The local authority now had to assess whether Ruby, who had not been able to hold on to her own daughter, could be a safe carer for her granddaughter.

There is another very basic difference between giving kinship care and applying to an agency to become a foster carer. The decision to become a kinship carer has not been planned, but invariably made in response to the circumstances of a known child or children. This poses more questions:

- Do you have the space in your home and in your life to accommodate children? How will children fit into your life style and life plans? If sisters or brothers need to stay together, can you accommodate another one now or later? What about retirement, health problems and stamina?

> **I told them I'd take all three children. There was never any doubt about that. But I said to them: 'You've got to help me with childminding and holidays, I've got a life and I'm going to keep it, or I'd be no good to them or to me.'**
> (45-year-old grandmother)

- What financial and other support might you need? Can you ask for help, and whom would you ask?
- Will you need to change your job? How will your employer view extra time off? How will your employment rights be affected?
- What childcare arrangements will you need to make?
- How do you feel about changing childcare practices, especially discipline, punishment and openness?
- How prepared are you for the developmental stages of childhood, adolescence and independence?
- What is your attitude towards impairment, learning disability, education, health, ethnicity and anything else you consider relevant?
- Which kind of kinship care arrangement would suit you and this child, or these children, in this particular situation? How do you feel about having, not having, or sharing parental responsibility?
- What will happen if you become sick or die, if the local authority does not share parental responsibility?

These lists may sound alarming, but it is common sense that kinship carers should look as much as they can before they leap. Even if you are caring for children on an entirely private basis, you may find it helpful to ask yourself many of these questions.

If you have been assessed and turned down by the local authority, it does not mean that you are unfit to look after a child, but it may be thought that you are unable to meet some particular needs or that a kinship placement might be damaging to you and your immediate family. All such decisions should be discussed with you, and you can appeal against them if you disagree. Every local authority has a complaints procedure but it is best to speak to a senior social worker before making an official complaint.

> Ruby, above, was assessed by her local authority and turned down as a kinship carer for her baby granddaughter. The reason given was that although she was doing well enough now, the extra burden of parenting again might upset the balance for the whole family. Ruby disagreed and said so. A second assessment, by a more experienced worker, recommended that the baby should be placed with her as a foster child under a Care Order to be reviewed after one year. This gave the local authority the right to monitor, and the duty to support the placement.

Every adult who looks after a child formally, or who lives in the same household as the child, will be asked to agree to:

- criminal record checks;
- health enquiries supported by a medical report; and
- social services record checks.

What matters is not having an absolutely clean sheet, but being able to keep a child safe.

11

What kind of support is available?

JOHN BIRDSALL PHOTOGRAPHY POSED BY MODELS

Support is a network of people you know you can call on...they are just there...even if you don't ever actually need them.
(Quoted in O'Neill, 2003)

Everyone needs support. Most of us muddle through with the casual and often unremarked support of friends, family and colleagues. When people become kinship carers, support becomes more urgent and more serious. With luck, the whole network will rally round. But there are some instances when outside help is necessary and it is important to know what is available, how to ask for it and how to find what is right for you.

Support is as good as it feels. Support has to be useful and useable. Support offered with good intentions by the giver is not supportive if the receiver finds it unhelpful. Social work support can feel like an intrusion if you think you are being "watched", or like a reliable lifeline if it is built on trust. Until recently, kinship carers have largely been "invisible" and have probably assumed that they won't need services or won't get them or both; once a child was re-established in the family, little formal support was offered. Legislation now makes it clear that support has to be based on the needs of the child and carers, not on the status of the placement, and that kinship carers have a right to all family placement support services. According to kinship carers, there is a "service gap" and customised services for kinship placements are still rare, but there is a growing awareness of kinship support needs; all family and friends carers should be given clear, written information about local authority policy and practice, which ought to cover the following.

- **Managing relationships in the family**
  Children will change their views of relatives if grandparents, aunts or uncles take on the role of their parents. Grandparents sometimes say that they have had to sacrifice their "fun" relationship with their grandchildren in order to be full-time carers. If you are the primary carer, consistency and discipline become more important. Other grandchildren may feel jealous of the sister, brother or cousin now living with their grandma. Aunts and uncles may find that their own children are resentful when a cousin becomes a sort of brother. The parents of the child may feel ousted from the family if they have

misused drugs or alcohol, or if they have harmed or neglected their child, and it can be devastating for the whole family to be faced with evidence of abuse.

> Sindy fostered her nephew when her sister became mentally unstable and harmed her son. Sindy had always relied on their mother and the two women had enjoyed spending time together. But now her mother couldn't believe that one of her daughters would abuse her own child and she blamed Sindy for taking the boy from his mother. This made it hard for Sindy to visit as before, and so she lost her chief means of support when she most needed it. A local authority social worker was able to help Sindy's mother to understand and accept what had happened.

- **Managing contact arrangements**
  If contact between children and their parents and other family members can be casual and left to happen as it will, and if everyone feels happy about it, then there is no problem. But it isn't always easy to be as flexible as one would like to be. There could be Court Orders or Children's Hearing Orders limiting or preventing contact with certain people. There could be hostility between the mother's and the father's sides of the family or, as is not uncommon, between the mother and the father. The children may be asking for more contact than you think wise or refusing to have contact altogether. Keeping in touch with siblings who have remained with their parents, or have been placed elsewhere could be tricky if there is conflict and rivalry. You may wish contact to be in a more neutral place than your home or you may want someone else to be in charge when parents visit. You will certainly want to be clear whether you are supposed to be supervising the contact, supporting the parents, protecting the child, or just enjoying the visits.

Peter, a widower, looked after his teenage grandson on an informal basis. Both parents were drug users. They visited their son erratically and often behaved in a bizarre manner. They were known to social services and Peter asked their social worker to control the contact. The parents really didn't mean to upset their son and an agreement was negotiated. Regular contact would take place at the nearby Family Centre and would be supervised by one of the Centre workers. If the parents arrived late or in a drugged state, they would not see their son. If they arrived at Peter's house uninvited, he would not let them in.

This agreement was reached without invoking the law. Sometimes decisions can best be made with the help of an independent mediator or a social worker experienced in family group conferencing. And sometimes it is necessary to have good advice about applying to the court for legal backing to protect the child and yourself.

• Behaviour difficulties

Children who cannot live at home because their parents are dead or sick or children who feel rejected, or who have been neglected or abused, will communicate their pain through their behaviour. We may say that their behaviour is the message – it tells us how they feel about themselves and the situation they are in. Even if children stay within their own family circle, they will at least have experienced separation and sorrow. They will probably be angry about the separation and they may make you the target of their rage. Very often a child's emotional development is arrested by bad experiences. Lying, stealing, bed-wetting, unprovoked anger and aggression or complete withdrawal may be symptoms of distress and cries for help. Behaviour that is not exceptional for a three-year-old can be hard to accept from an older child.

> **Angie used to be such a lovely little girl when she came to see us. She was bright and loving and very polite. Since she's come to live with us we've seen a different side of her. She's sullen and rude and sometimes we think we can't go on like this.**
> (Grandparents of six-year-old girl)

Advice should be available from social services about where you can seek help. Some social workers are specially trained to ease children through difficult phases. There are also therapeutic agencies that can work with the child in more serious cases and parenting programmes that can suggest ways of approaching behaviour problems. You don't have to wait until there is a crisis before getting support.

- **Sharing duties and responsibilities**
Unless you are the only person with parental responsibility (responsibilities in Scotland), you will be sharing it with at least one parent or perhaps both. If you are fostering or looking after a related child informally, you may not have any legal claim at all to act on behalf of the child. However, most foster carers and informal carers are expected to make the day-to-day decisions in a common sense sort of way. Sharing responsibility with parents can be a positive arrangement for all concerned if it works. The parents demonstrate trust in the carer's ability; the carer shows respect for the parents' views; the child knows that the parents are still involved and sees that adults can co-operate.

If shared responsibility cannot be worked out in a friendly manner, more formal agreements may have to be made with the assistance of social services or a voluntary agency specialising in kinship care (see Useful organisations). Who will have control regarding medical treatments, education, school outings, holidays, pocket money, presents, overnight stays, body piercing, designer labels and any other questions that may arise? Agreements can be made right at the beginning of a kinship placement, but more often difficulties emerge later on.

> **After my niece first came to live with me, her mum used to turn up with expensive presents and give her money like a fairy godmother. And she interfered with our plans because she never even let us know she was in the country, let alone coming to see us. It led to arguments in front of Martina, which wasn't good for any of us. So we asked Martina's social worker to sort it out. She made an agreement we all signed and it's been OK. Martina's mum has responsibility for buying all her clothes and she sends her pocket money every month. I'm in charge of everything else – it suits me because I hate shopping and they love it.**
> (Aunt of 12-year-old girl)

> **We took the baby straight from hospital and we never even met the mother. Then we didn't see or hear from our son for 17 years. We brought her up on a Residence Order without help from anybody. Now our son's marched back in with a glamorous new wife and a good job and a better house than we've got. She's at the age when she's rebelling anyway and she's making her dad into an idol. We're getting written out. It's heartbreaking. He has parental rights and we don't since she turned 16. We need someone to mediate for the sake of our granddaughter.**
> (Request to Grandparents Plus)

- **Disability**

  A disabled child may have a variety of special needs. Having easy access to expert advice and specialists can smooth the way for carers. All disabled children have a right to services and should have a named social worker.

  > **He should have done better at school though he's disabled. I needed more help with it.**
  > (Grandparent carer)

- **Substance misuse**

  If someone in your family misuses drugs or alcohol, and you take on the role of carer for their children, you may feel angry or resentful about their habit and uncertain about the physical and emotional effect on the children. Your GP will be able to advise whether the children need to be referred to a specialist agency. Adfam (see Useful organisations) can advise about support groups for the relatives of drug users.

  > **It was a real eye-opener hearing other people's stories, it made me realise how much in denial I was. I decided not to lie when Jacob asks me things. I would rather he hears it from me: 'Some drugs are good and some drugs are bad. Mummy takes drugs that are bad.'**
  > (Jacob's grandmother quoted in Adfam, 2004)

- **Managing stress**

  Most parents get stressed out at some time or another. You only have to listen to parents talking by the school gates to know that parenthood has its ups and downs. It relieves the stress if relatives and friends are on hand to give the children treats and the parents short breaks. If available relatives are already providing full-time care, is there anyone else who will

take the children for an afternoon, a weekend, an outing?
Mothers frequently form groups to support each other. They
meet in each other's houses with their children, they babysit
for each other, and they confide in each other. Kinship carers,
especially if they are older, may not fit easily into this pattern.

> One grandmother said that she couldn't afford to pay a
> babysitter and felt too exhausted to offer babysitting in return.

There are usually support groups and training events available
for foster carers, but kinship carers who foster may not feel
comfortable sharing their experiences with carers who are
unrelated to their foster children.

> An aunt, who looked after her brother's three children, formed
> her own support group. She invited all the family to tea once a
> month and used the opportunity to discuss the children's
> progress and to see who wanted to help out where and when.
> This made the children feel connected to the wider family and
> gave the aunt some built-in respite.

Grandparents have found it helpful to meet in groups with
other grandparents giving kinship care. However much you try
to be realistic about what it might be like to parent again, no
one can be fully prepared before it happens. Whether you give
up work, forego leisure in retirement, or juggle employment
and childcare, it is good to be able to tell it as it is, to people
who know what you are talking about: people who will
understand how it feels if grandchildren have been harmed or
neglected by other family members; people who will share the
experience of divided loyalties between their own children and
their grandchildren.

With luck, your local authority will be able to offer a
support group for kinship carers or for grandparent carers in

particular. If they can't, you might be the person to inspire them to get a group going. Or you could enquire from the Family Rights Group or Grandparents' Association (see Useful organisations) whether there is an existing kinship carers group in your vicinity. If all else fails, you may add a new dimension to an existing foster carer's support group.

Looking after needy children can take its toll; you have to look after yourself as well, by making sure that you are not left to go it alone.

- **Money matters**
  Looking after children and yourself can cost a surprising amount of money. If children have an impairment or some special needs, it can cost more. Don't ever let anyone tell you that families should look after their own for love alone. Currently there is no specific benefit or allowance for grandparents or other kinship carers but family and friends are entitled to the same state benefits as parents because they are paid to the person looking after the child. However, carers have reported difficulty in claiming allowances if the parents are still drawing Child Benefit. The process of switching payments from a parent to a carer can take time.

  Some local authorities have a Welfare Rights Officer who can steer carers through the maze of available financial support.
  * *Child Benefit*. This is not means-tested and is payable for every child up to the age of 16, or 19 if the young person is studying for more than 12 hours a week. You do not have to be the parent to receive this benefit but you must be able to provide evidence that the child is living with you.
  * *Tax Credits*. These are means-tested and depend on your earnings as well as childcare commitments.
  * *Income Support and Minimum Income Guarantee*. This is linked to your pensions and other income and may lead to further benefits such as mortgage interest payments, council

tax and housing benefits. If you have had to give up work in order to care for a child, and you are worried that your pension will be reduced as a result, you may be entitled to "home responsibility protection".

* *Disability Benefits*. Several allowances and grants are available depending on the severity of the impairment. You can get details from your local Citizen's Advice Bureau or GP, or you can ring one of the helplines listed in Useful organisations.

* *Foster Care Allowance*. All foster carers are paid to maintain the children who live with them and also qualify for grants to cover equipment, holidays and extra needs. Kinship carers who foster should be paid at the same rate as non-related local authority carers. The level and national conformity of payments, and the inclusion of a "reward element" are currently under review.

* *Adoption Allowance*. Adopters can be paid a means-tested allowance by their local authority if adoption is in the child's best interests, and financial support is required to secure the adoption.

* *Guardian's Allowance*. People who have been named as a child's legal guardian can claim this state benefit.

* *Residence Order Allowance* and *Special Guardianship Allowance*. These are not paid as of right, but can be negotiated with the local authority according to need. They are generally set at a lower level than fostering allowances but can be enhanced in special circumstances.

* *Special grants*. Your local social services department can meet the needs of children by giving special grants to enable a child, who is not fostered, to remain in the family. They could pay for transport costs, school uniforms, baby equipment, beds and bedding, and even, in some cases, for building work and alterations.

As well as your social services department, some charities and government schemes may also be able to offer financial

support. Sure Start is a government initiative that can help
with childcare. Some voluntary organisations can make
grants for specific purposes. You can get more information
from the Citizen's Advice Bureau or from the internet.

- **Moving on**
  If a kinship placement has to end, there may be sadness and
  resentment. Organising a move to other carers will require
  support from the rest of the family and from professionals. If
  the child returns to his or her parents prematurely, there may
  be conflict and even danger for the child. It's best to give a
  loud cry for help before a situation becomes an emergency.

  When there is a planned move back to the child's parents,
  you and the child may need help to manage the transition and
  to ensure continuity. It will be as important for you to maintain
  contact with the child, as it was to remain in touch with the
  parents, while the child lived with you.

In general

Support for every citizen is built into the mainstream health,
education and community services. It is up to us how we use them.
Wanting and needing support as a kinship carer is not the same as
being unable to manage.

A lone grandfather taking on the care of three children under
10 said 'I'll manage' to every question the helpful social worker
put to him. He did indeed manage, but in due course he
needed support from family, friends, social services and the
education department in order to get more suitable
accommodation, to sort out the children's schooling, to oversee
health and dental checks, to buy clothes and equipment, and to
make adequate financial arrangements. He was a wonderful
grandfather and the children thrived.

Kinship carers manage in the most amazing circumstances. They don't always conform to a prescribed notion of how to manage, and they may not use support in the conventional way, but as the next section shows, it would be better if support were readily available.

12

A kinship care story

This is a real kinship network story. The grandparents raised their foster daughter from babyhood while she remained in care to the local authority. They "saved" her children from public care and brought them up as their own grandchildren. They have an extended family made up of permanent foster children, now adults, a "home-grown" son, children who have moved on to be adopted and numerous blood relatives. Kinship is what you make it, and so is kinship care.

| Chris Leaves' story

1982 was a momentous year for our family. My husband and I both worked full time. He worked long hours and travelled many miles for a finance company. I was a social worker for the local authority, and worked in a family centre.

We had been foster carers since we married in 1963. We had two permanent foster children, a girl and a boy, a son of our own and a terminally ill African Caribbean foster child who attended a school for disabled children.

Our foster daughter had married and left home the previous year, so we just had the three boys with us. Our youngest son was applying for the police force, and our eldest was planning to buy a house nearby. He was in his thirties by then, and we could not quite believe it would happen.

After two long years of very poor health our little foster son died. A few days later, our youngest son got his call to join the Metropolitan Police cadets at Hendon, and our eldest son exchanged contracts on his house. Phew! As you can imagine, we were somewhat dazed! Then our daughter gave birth to a little girl, and we were delighted to have our first grandchild. I should mention that our daughter has learning difficulties, as does her husband, so we were aware they would always need our support, but they lived close by, and we were happy to help.

So there we were, rattling around in our four-bedroomed house, thinking we had finally reached "Derby and Joan" status. There was concern that my husband's father was on his own, and not coping too well, so we planned to bring him to Peterborough to live near us, in due course.

Meanwhile we worked hard, enjoyed a couple of "Derby and Joan" holidays, occasionally ate out, spent time in our garden (one love of my life), and enjoyed our church activities and our many friends.

We did of course see a great deal of our little granddaughter, who was delightful, and our daughter proved to be an excellent mum, even though her husband was not a hands-on dad.

So life for three years was very different, but we were getting used to it. We continued fostering, just short-term or emergency placements.

Then in 1985 our second granddaughter was born. Things started to go badly wrong for our daughter and her husband. We were not sure whether it was one baby too many, but they were not coping. The older child had chicken pox, and after much deliberation our daughter asked if we could take the baby for a few days, as she had a poorly toddler, and they were all very tired. So we did. She stayed for several weeks, and however hard we tried they kept putting off having her back. That really was the start of many years of the children "to-ing" and "fro-ing" between their parents and us. As a social worker I was used to planning and negotiating with families – but how much more difficult when it is your own family. I have to say that the paternal grandparents were not helpful at this time, although I think they struggled to understand the situation.

We took the girls on holidays, clothed them, and paid for their parents to take them away as well. The girls settled well at school, and we took them to out-of-school activities to try to make their life as normal as possible. Our daughter's mental health was not good, and her husband and in-laws could not get to grips with this at all. From 1985 until 1990 the girls moved in and out of our home, while we tried to get our daughter well enough to cope with her family.

In 1990 she was sectioned under the Mental Health Act, and the girls moved in with us again, as their dad could not cope with working and looking after them. Over the next year our daughter did not improve and we were concerned at the lack of interest their father showed in the girls, although he did visit our daughter regularly.

Taking the girls to see her was soul-destroying, and we felt torn between them all. Eventually our daughter quite suddenly announced she was divorcing her husband. It came totally out of the blue for us, and for him, and he came and removed the children in a fit of rage.

Then began 18 months of hell. Their father refused us and our daughter any contact with the children, and because they lived nearby, we would see them sad, and poorly cared for. We did not know where to turn. I had not confided in many colleagues, choosing to keep my professional life separate. Eventually we got a solicitor, went to court, and finally got spasmodic contact.

This was a terrible time, as the girls begged us not to take them back to Dad, but we were terrified to do anything that would be seen as wrong by the court in case we jeopardised our daughter's rights. Our daughter was not getting any better and she was desperate not to return to her former home. We attempted to help her find somewhere to live, so that we could support her with the girls as we had always done.

Our son-in-law qualified for legal aid whilst we had to pay our solicitor. The solicitor's fees were frightening as we had to return to court many times to hear our son-in-law promise to allow us contact, and then go back to court again when he went back on his word. Eventually, after 18 months, we were granted a Residence Order, and the children's father walked from the court saying he did not want to see his children again. We tried to negotiate with him, but by then he had found a new partner who had two girls the same age as his own, and it was fraught with difficulties. Our older granddaughter did visit a few times, and was desperate to see him, but the youngest would have nothing to do with him, however hard we tried.

Meanwhile, as soon as the children moved in, our daughter made a remarkable recovery, and was re-housed in a flat nearby.

So life for us took another turn, and we got on with the job of bringing up our two granddaughters. The girls were 10 and seven by this time, and their mother recovered well enough to be able to care for them before and after school, and we used childminders for the long school holidays so that I could continue to work. We only had Child Benefit, and have never received payment from either parent. The children grew up with us by private arrangement.

We found activities to boost our granddaughters' self-esteem, struggled through the homework, and went on child-centred holidays again. My husband's father moved into the house with us for a year, whilst an annexe was built. Three generations, but it worked OK. Unfortunately, ten days after the builders left, he died, but his annexe has made an excellent independent flat for our eldest granddaughter.

Our daughter saw the girls daily, and they were able to spend a night at her flat occasionally. We had a tough time changing from "doting grandparent" to "authoratitive parenting" roles, and also making sure that the girls were not playing one adult off against the other. At the end of the day we were in charge. I have to say our daughter accepted this well. With hindsight I realise that since her illness she finds it hard to make any decision and will opt out readily.

How hard was it?

I suppose the most painful thing initially was how badly my daughter's husband and her in-laws treated her during her illness, and indeed my husband and me, when we were desperately trying to do what was best for the girls. The verbal abuse and humiliation were intolerable.

The length of time the court case took, and the cost, was unbelievable.

The girls left the court in what they were wearing, and any clothes we were later able to retrieve had to be binned. The majority of their toys, photographs, etc, were destroyed by their father, who set fire to them.

The court did try to get some mediation for us, but the children's father would not engage.

A weekly payment would have been a tremendous help, or an initial payment to provide new uniforms, beds, or a bike.

| **What helped?**

We were very lucky in having a good supportive family, and lots of friends and colleagues, who offered listening ears and shoulders to cry on.

We were able to continue working to ease the financial burden.

I learned of the Grandparents' Association, and got in touch with them, and they really understood our situation. I have also done work with the Family Rights Group and with Grandparents Plus. They have been an inspiration to me, and are doing all they can to raise awareness with politicians and policy makers on "grandparenting issues"

| **So what has been the outcome?**

Well, we are very proud of our two granddaughters. They are now 22 and 19. The eldest is a manager in a local garden centre, has joined the local constabulary as a "special constable", drives a car, and enjoys spending time on her computer. The youngest is an admin assistant in a local firm. She too drives, has a steady boyfriend, and enjoys music.

Their mother has almost recovered her health, and copes well in her own home. We see her every week; her relationship with the girls is similar to many teenagers, "as and when it suits".

Their father still lives with his partner nearby, and we occasionally see him in the town. Both girls would like to have some contact with him, but recently he told the older girl he was not ready to see them, and his partner would not approve. It is ironic that after his "tale of woe" his daughter said, 'Poor Dad, he's not up to it'. Our youngest granddaughter, who has consistently refused to have any contact, is now desperate to see him. She has so much anger in her, I fear for him!

So what about us?

Well, when my husband retired six years ago we continued our fostering, believing it would be good for the girls. It worked very well, and we had five more placements before I retired. That was the end of an era for us, 40 years of fostering. All of our latter placements were for pre-adoption, and those children have continued to be very much part of our large extended family.

We have learnt so much the "second time around". Yes, we have also been tired, hard up, and longed for some time for ourselves.

We knew of no others in our situation until I began to receive referrals at work about grandparents caring for grandchildren, and needing nursery provision. I have set up an independent support group here in Peterborough for grandparents who are raising their grandchildren, and it has been running for 10 years now. What a wonderful group of people they are, selfless in their efforts to do the very best for their grandchildren. We all help each other, offering support where needed because we know "how it is".

Our youngest son and his wife have blessed us with another granddaughter. You see there is justice in this world, because we now have all the time we want for her, and see her regularly. She comes to stay, and we are able to hand her back, and enjoy the "doting" role again.

We are of course the "new age" grandparents who understand (within limitations) modern technology. We can fax, email, text, and know our way round websites. We know about the latest pop groups, and are ashamed to say we know all the words to Busted's latest album. We know the "in" speak, where the clubs and pubs are, and know where to hide when collecting the girls from such places.

We have done our best to ensure our granddaughters have grown up in their family of origin – they know about their own and their mother's heritage – and we are richer (not financially!) for having done so. The only other alternative would have been for them to have been brought up in the care of the local authority or, as in many cases, to be adopted, and chances are, we would have had contact severed.

Chris Leaves, January 2005

A young person's view

Clare, the older of the two granddaughters above, didn't want to write her side of the kinship care story, but she agreed to write answers to questions suggested by her grandmother.

What can you remember about living with Mum and Dad?

I remember the night Mum got sectioned. I remember Dad was always off working so we didn't see him too much. Mum usually picked us up from school and I remember one day when we got home from school, Dad came home with a broken arm.

I remember driving in the car with Nan going to visit Mum and Helen in hospital. When we got there, Mum was sitting in the chair and Helen was in her cot. I gave Helen a small pink teddy as a present.

I remember when Dad was looking after us at home and when Helen and I went to bed, I always used to sneak downstairs and sit with him – making sure Helen was asleep so she couldn't take up my time with Dad.

When Helen was being naughty I used to get the blame for it and when we were arguing I got the blame all the time. I think we used to argue a lot – I don't think we were ever that close when we were younger.

What can you remember about the break-up and Mum's illness?

I didn't know much about Mum's illness before it happened – we were staying with Nan and Grandad for about a week or so before, and I remember saying to them that I wanted to go home and see Mum and Dad.

I slept in Helen's room and heard some shouting downstairs so I went down to see what was up and Mum was sitting in the chair in the kitchen – rocking – Dad was there.

I went into the kitchen and the doctor came and next thing I remember Grandad was there. I went back up to Helen's room (Helen was still with Nan) and Grandad was knocking on the door trying to get in. I was standing behind not letting him in, telling him to 'go away'. The next thing I know I was at Nanny Carol's that night.

The next morning Nan arrived at the house with Helen and we both had the day off school so we went to Nan's nursery. Mum was in hospital. At the beginning we weren't allowed to see her – I think it was to find out if she was affected by me and Helen. I can't remember who looked after us – it was either of the grandparents. We did eventually go and see Mum (a few weeks or a month later) and I remember her being really happy to see us. I think she was pacing the floors when we got there and one of the nurses said, 'Look who's here to see you!'

We didn't really know what happened until years later when we sat down and spoke to Nan and Grandad about it. We lived with Dad for a bit when Mum was in hospital. Then Dad started to bring

Elaine around to the house and we spent a couple of nights at her house. Then he began to shift all our gear over to her place, and when we stayed there we had to sleep on the floor, as she had two kids as well. Once when Helen and I were alone with Elaine and we had spaghetti bolognese, Helen accidentally spilled all her food on the floor, and Elaine picked it off the floor and put it back on the plate and ordered Helen to eat it – it was full of hairs. Helen refused so she went without any food that night.

When Mum was in a group home she used to come back to stay with Nan and Grandad – I never wanted to leave Dad and go with Mum – I don't know why I felt like that.

I think it wasn't until the court hearing that I realized that Mum and Dad had actually broken up. I felt confused and upset that they were not going to live together again.

What about when you went to live with Nan and Grandad?

When I was sitting in the waiting room at the court with this official court guy, he asked us, 'Who do you want to live with?' and Helen replied, 'I want to live with Nan and I want to live with her now!' and then he asked me and I said, 'I don't know'. Dad used to always say, 'Wherever Helen goes, you go – I don't want you two split up'. The court guy said, 'I can't guarantee that you will go with your Nan and Grandad today.'

I remember sitting in the court cafeteria with Grandad and finishing our drinks and sandwiches and he said, 'Come on, let's go find Nan'. I saw Mum walking down the stairs in tears with Nan by her side. Dad and Elaine went storming out of the court and I remember asking, 'Where's Daddy going?' Mum said, 'You're coming to live with us now', and I gave her a big hug. I remember travelling back in the car to Nan and Grandad's. I was feeling happy that I didn't have to live with Elaine again and pleased that Helen and I were staying together.

That weekend Grandad dropped me and Helen off with Mum at the fair and we had a great time. Grandad came to pick us up and took us home again and when we walked into the house loads of people jumped up and shouted 'Surprise!' Nan and Grandad had a Welcome Home party for us.

Helen and I used to share the same room, and if we didn't go to bed at the same time, Helen would stay awake until I came up and we used to chat and play. Grandad sometimes had to come up and threaten to slap our bums with his slipper! He always got Helen's bum but I managed to move quicker than she did so he rarely got mine!

I used to go around every Saturday and see Nanny Carol – Nan used to drop me off – sometimes Dad came over with Elaine but he never really talked to me. I used to go out and play with one of the girls over the road. I do wish I could have seen him more.

Once when I went round to Nanny Carol's, I overheard her saying to one of her friends on the phone that she had a 'tumour'. I called Nan up from a call box and told her what I heard – nothing else was really said about it. I think Nanny Carol just wanted to forget all about it. I think it was the following Friday – it was Children in Need and we were allowed to stay up late – I think we went to bed at about 10.45. About 11 Nan came upstairs and told us Nanny Carol had died.

I know that during the week I called Dad up and said I wanted to go to the funeral – he was fine and told me the time, etc. I think Nan and Grandad dropped me off outside Nanny Carol's house – I was wearing a Peterborough United scarf that Nanny Carol had bought me but Dad told me to take it off.

I sat next to Grandad Dave in the crematorium, which wasn't fair because he was so upset – I thought Dad should have sat there. I was about 12 or 13 at the time.

When we went outside to see the flowers, Elaine gave me a hug but I don't recall Dad hugging me. Grandad Dave said we will always stay in touch and to come and visit, and Dad said the same – but I haven't seen Grandad Dave for nine years.

We did attempt to get in contact with Grandad Dave – I rang him up to arrange for me and Helen to go around and see him. We went around to his house but there was no answer so we went round to Dad's to see if he was there. Dad walked us back to Grandad Dave's with the dog. On the way there, Dad started hitting Max (the dog) with a stick – not a friendly hit but a whack – I told him to stop but he said, 'It is the only way he'll behave'. I think that was the last proper time we actually spent with Dad – we never did get to see Grandad Dave – he's moved house since. I did ask Grandad if he could find out where he lived, which he did. I posted something through his door, but never got any reply back.

One other time I saw Dad I passed him in the street and he didn't even recognize me – I shouted, 'Dad', and he didn't respond so I shouted, 'Philip', and he turned round. He was always upset when we met, saying things like, 'I've always loved you and Helen and never stopped loving your Mum', etc. I know Helen and I have written him loads of letters and tried calling him but he has never replied, or Elaine always answered the phone.

On one occasion I had just passed my driving test and Helen wanted to go and see Dad – Helen got out but I stayed in the car. Elaine answered the door and said he wasn't there – then we went home again. The following night Elaine called the house and spoke to Nan for an hour or so, saying something along the lines of, 'If they call again we will call the police'. Nan was saying to her, 'You've got kids, think how they would feel'. We didn't bother to try and contact him again. I see Grandad more as my Dad than Philip – I don't think I even love him.

What do you wish could have happened?

Mum and Dad staying together, me and Helen growing up – just like a normal family.

Did you feel different from other children?

It felt like the norm to me.

If the teachers referred to my "parents" I would correct them – and they would say "grandparents", and not ask why, or bat an eyelid!

I told the other children my dad had cleared off with another woman, and my mum was not capable of looking after us, because of her illness.

Some of my friends thought my grandparents were really cool and envied us, because we went on holidays abroad, had the latest gear, and a comfortable lifestyle.

I have not had any problem with my grandparents being older. I seriously think we have had a more secure life with Nan and Grandad than if we had stayed with Mum and Dad.

Could anyone have done anything to make life easier for you and Helen?

Elaine could have let us share their beds.

Dad and Grandad Dave could have kept in touch.

Nan and Grandad couldn't have made it any easier than they did – they were great.

Do you think your experiences have influenced how you may handle relationships in the future?

I think I probably hold back quite a bit when it comes to friends – I don't trust easily – it takes me a while to get used to people. I don't like talking to new people and know I should socialise but it makes me feel uncomfortable. I was bullied throughout my school years as well, so that has knocked my confidence even more. If anyone is peeing me off, I take it to heart. If it's in the work environment, then I put them straight. Work gives me the confidence I need.

> **If you could wave a magic wand, what would you wish for right now?**

I think everything happens for a reason, so I wouldn't want to change my past as I've been happy living with Nan and Grandad. I wish Dad bothered more about us to actually make an effort. I wish for Mum to be happy and to meet a new bloke and if she's happy being on her own, I'm happy for her too.

Clare, January 2005

Readers will be able to make their own connections between these stories and the various sections of this book.

Note about the contributors

Chris Leaves and her husband, Colin, were long-term foster carers for 40 years and have been kinship carers for two of their grandchildren – the daughters of their foster daughter. Chris first trained as a nursery nurse and later as a social worker. She has worked with children and families for nearly 50 years. She set up and still runs the Second Generation support group for kinship carers in Peterborough.

Clare is Chris and Colin's granddaughter.

13

And finally . . . good advice

JOHN BIRDSALL PHOTOGRAPHY POSED BY MODELS

When you get older, you can see things more clearly, you have more patience and more time.
(Grandparent quoted in Broad *et al*, 2001)

The following advice has been adapted from the messages kinship carers have sent out from support groups and interviews (with thanks to David Pitcher and Bob Broad).

- Make sure you understand the social services system. Don't wait until you need them to find out how they can help.
- If you do not have an allocated social worker, there should be a named person to ask for.
- If you foster, sort out at the beginning what your rights and responsibilities are, and what social services will do.
- If you need help with housing, transport, or money, ask for it. You're not supposed to be a cheap option.
- Get the support of the rest of the family; don't try and do it on your own.
- Don't do it if you're not confident or wholly committed. Don't do it just to keep the family happy.
- Be clear what you are offering. If it's childminding, don't let yourself be persuaded to take on full-time care.
- If you take one or two children it doesn't mean you can as easily take three or four.
- Don't feel guilty if you can't do it – there are other ways of helping your family.
- Don't forget who the parents are: treat the children as your own, but never forget that they're not.
- Remember there are two sides to every family; the child has relations on the mother's and the father's side.
- You can't wipe out what's happened but you can talk about it.
- Don't ever blame the child for what the parents did.
- Get a legal order and social services support if you need to protect yourself or the children.
- Pay attention to education – my granddaughter missed two years of education. I got her back into school. Now she's taking five GCSEs.
- If you're going to play football at the weekends, expect to feel knackered.

- Enjoy keeping up with the latest trends – it may keep you feeling young.
- Make a will: you may not live forever!
- Don't be a martyr: the child will benefit if you look after yourself.
- Being a kinship carer can make you stop and look at yourself in a way you wouldn't normally.
- You can give the best support to other kinship carers. You could offer your services to your local authority.
- You can't force children who don't want to come. It's got to be their choice.
- **...You might get a few hiccups with them, but life is full of hiccups.**

The last words must go to a young woman brought up in kinship care:

> **My gran, she's 100 per cent, she's been our rock and kept the whole family together. If it wasn't for her we'd probably all be separated and not grown up with each other... I wouldn't be the stable person I am today if it wasn't for my gran.**

References

Adfam (2004) *Journeys: Living with a partner using drugs*, London: Adfam

Broad B, Hayes R and Rushforth C (2001) *Kith and Kin: Kinship care for vulnerable young people*, London: National Children's Bureau

Broad B (ed) (2001) *Kinship Care: The placement choice for children and young people*, Lyme Regis: Russell House Publishing

McFadden E J (1995) *Family Traditions: Kinship caregivers' forums*, Michigan: Eastern Michigan University

O'Neill C (2003) 'The simplicity and complexity of support', in Argent H (ed) *Staying Connected*, London: BAAF

Pitcher D (1999) *When Grandparents Care*, Plymouth: Plymouth Council

Rowe J, Cain H, Hundleby M and Keane A (1984) *Long-Term Foster Care*, London: Batsford/BAAF

Useful organisations

Adfam
A national organisation that supports families when they have drug or alcohol problems.
Waterbridge House
32–36 Loman Street
London SE1 0EH
Tel: 020 7928 8898
www.adfam.org.uk

British Association for Adoption and Fostering (BAAF)
A UK-wide organisation for everyone involved in adoption, fostering and childcare. Provides a wide range of publications for carers and professionals.
Head Office
Skyline House
200 Union Street
London SE1 0LX
Tel: 020 7593 2000
www.baaf.org.uk

BAAF Scotland
40 Shandwick Place
Edinburgh EH2 4RT
Tel: 0131 220 4749

BAAF Cymru
7 Cleeve House
Lambourne Crescent
Cardiff CF14 5GP
Tel: 029 2076 1155

Children in Scotland
The national agency for all organisations and individuals working with children and their families in Scotland.
Princess House
5 Shandwick Place
Edinburgh
EH12 4RG
Tel: 0131 228 8484
www.childreninscotland.org.uk

Contact a Family
Provides support, advice and information for carers of children with disabilities, and helps to put families in touch with each other.
209–211 City Road
London EC1V 1JN
Tel: 020 7608 8700
www.cafamily.org.uk

Family Rights Group
A national organisation that advises on family law and childcare practice, with a special interest in kinship care.
The Print House
18 Ashwin Court
London E8 3DL
Tel: 020 7923 2628
www.frg.org.uk

Fostering Network
A membership organisation for everyone involved in fostering. It provides a 24-hour legal advice service.
Head Office
87 Blackfriars Road
London SE1 8HA
Tel: 020 7620 6400
www.fostering.net

Fostering Network in Scotland
2nd Floor Ingram House
227 Ingram Street
Glasgow G1 1DA
Tel: 0141 204 1400

Fostering Network in Wales
Suite 11, 2nd Floor
Bay Chambers
West Bute Street
Cardiff Bay CF10 5BB
Tel: 029 2044 0940

Grandparents' Association
A self-help group supporting grandparents.
Moot House
The Stow, Harlow
Essex CH20 3AG
Tel: 01279 444964
www.grandparents-association.org.uk

Grandparents plus
A national organisation that offers consultation and training for grandparents as well as other relatives and professionals.
18 Victoria Park Square
Bethnal Green
London E2 9PF
Tel: 020 8981 8001
www.grandparentsplus.org.uk

| **Helplines**

The Child Benefit Centre Line: 0870 155 5540

The Disability Benefits Line: 0800 243355

The Minimum Income Guarantee Line: 0800 028 1111

The Pensions Information Line: 0845 731 3233

The Contact a Family Line (disability issues): 0808 808 3555

The Grandparents' Association Line: 01279 444964

Parentline Plus: email parentsupport@parentlineplus.org.uk

Useful resources

The books listed below are available from BAAF. Please visit www.baaf.org.uk or contact 020 7593 2072 to order or for further details.

| Books for adults

Henrietta Bond, *Fostering a Child*, BAAF, 2004
An ideal starting point for anyone considering becoming a foster carer, this book covers who can foster, who to approach if you want to apply, training and getting started, and fees and allowances. It includes a list of UK fostering agencies.

Henrietta Bond (ed), *'If you don't stick with me, who will?' The challenges and rewards of foster care*, BAAF, 2005
This collection of first-person accounts from foster carers tells what it's like to foster children and young people, many of whom have experienced loss, trauma, abuse or just a very difficult start in life, and explores the problems, challenges and rewards of foster care.

Kate Cairns, *Attachment, Trauma and Resilience*, BAAF, 2002
A beautifully written account of a personal and professional experience of living with children who have been hurt by their early experiences, which will be of interest to anyone living or working with troubled children.

Hope Massiah (ed), *Looking After our Own*, BAAF, 2005
This inspiring collection looks at the experiences of nine black and Asian adoptive families and their children, exploring their motivation to adopt, what their social workers had to offer and the roles of their families and friends. These absorbing stories offer pointers to what can make a successful adoption, and what to avoid.

Shaila Shah, *Fostering: What it is and what it means*, BAAF, 2003
In this short, brightly illustrated booklet, information about fostering including the process and procedures is clearly set out. Designed to be worked through with a child both before and after fostering.

| **Books for children**

Hedi Argent and Mary Lane, *What Happens in Court?*, BAAF, 2003
This user-friendly guide will help children understand the role that a court might play in their lives. It includes information on who's who in court, and the various court orders that can be made.

Hedi Argent, *What is a Disability?*, BAAF, 2004
With the understanding that every child is special and children with disabilities are more special in a different way, this colourful guide explains what disabilities are by telling the stories of some disabled children.

Jean Camis, *My Life and Me*, BAAF, 2001
A colourful interactive life story book designed to help children develop and record their memories, with spaces for writing, drawing and photographs. Guidelines are provided to help carers understand the significance of each section.

Jean Camis, *We are Fostering*, BAAF, 2003
This colourful workbook, designed for birth children in families that are fostering, will help birth children to know themselves and their role in the family, and to be prepared to welcome new arrivals into their homes and lives.

Angela Lidster, *Chester and Daisy Move On*, BAAF, 1999
This popular and engaging picture book is for use with children aged 4–10 who are moving on to adoption, to help them explore

feelings about their past and their moves, and to help carers identify these issues from the child's perspective.

Barbara Orritt, *Dennis Duckling*, **The Children's Society, 1999**
Dennis, an appealing little duckling, has to leave his parents as they can no longer look after him. He goes to live on a new pond where he is cared for by grown-up ducks. Suitable for use with children aged 4–8.

The Family Rights Group produces a selection of useful guides, advice sheets and videos, many of which would be of interest to kinship carers. For more information, visit www.frg.org.uk or telephone 020 7923 2628.